Prophets
and
Prophecy

SECRETS OF THE SUPERNATURAL

Prophets and Prophecy

REBECCA STEFOFF

Marshall Cavendish
Benchmark
New York

Marshall Cavendish Benchmark
99 White Plains Road
Tarrytown, New York 10591-9001
www.marshallcavendish.us

Library of Congress Cataloging-in-Publication Data
Stefoff, Rebecca
Prophets and prophecy / by Rebecca Stefoff.
p. cm. — Secrets of the supernatural)
Summary: "Explores the history, philosophy, and folklore surrounding
the concept of seeing the future"—Provided by publisher.
Includes bibliographical references and index.
ISBN 978-0-7614-2638-7
1. Prophecies—Juvenile literature. 2. Prophets—Juvenile literature. I. Title. II. Series.
BF1809.S74 2008
133.3—dc22
2007008779

Editor: Joyce Stanton
Publisher: Michelle Bisson
Art Director: Anahid Hamparian
Series Designer: Anne Scatto / PIXEL PRESS

Images provided by Rose Corbett Gordon, Art Editor, Mystic, CT, from the following sources:
Cover: Private Collection/The Maas Gallery, London/Bridgeman Art Library; *Back cover: The Illustrated London
News* Picture Library, London/Bridgeman Art Library; *pages 1, 2, 8, 22, 32, 39, 41, 42, 51, 61:* The Granger
Collection, NY; *pages 6, 40:* Roger-Viollet/The Image Works; *page 11:* Seat Archive/Alinari Archives/The
Image Works; *page 12:* Réunion des Musées Nationaux/Art Resource, NY; *pages 14, 71:* Ann Ronan Picture
Library/HIP/Art Resource, NY; *page 17:* Heiko Wolfraum/dpa/Corbis; *page 18:* Musée des Beaux-Arts, Rouen,
France/Lauros/Giraudon/Bridgeman Art Library; *page 21:* Francis G. Mayer/Corbis; *page 24:* Archive
Photos/Getty Images; *pages 26, 43:* Time Life Pictures/Getty Images; *page 27:* Bildarchiv Preussischer
Kulturbesitz/Art Resource, NY; *page 28:* Look and Learn, Private Collection/Bridgeman Art Library;
page 30: Brooklyn Museum/Corbis; *page 34:* Gary Bryan/Getty Images; *page 36:* English School/Getty Images;
page 37: Private Collection/Bridgeman Art Library; *page 38:* Scala/Art Resource, NY; *page 45:* Photomorgana/
Corbis; *page 46:* Bettmann/Corbis; *pages 49, 56:* Rue des Archives/The Granger Collection, New York;
pages 52, 55: Mary Evans Picture Library/The Image Works; *page 53:* Bibliothèque Nationale, Paris/
Lauros/Giraudon/Bridgeman Art Library; *page 58:* SV-Bilderdienst/The Image Works; *page 63:* Private
Collection/Look and Learn/Bridgeman Art Library; *pages 65, 68:* Topical Press Agency/Getty Images.

Printed in Malaysia

1   3   5   6   4   2

FRONT COVER: Cassandra, a mythical Greek prophetess
BACK COVER: Was the sinking of the *Titanic* foretold?
HALF TITLE: In the tarot deck, the Queen of Swords can represent a seer.
TITLE PAGE: *Angel of the Revelation*, painted around 1803 by British
   artist and poet William Blake

Contents

Two of the most famous prophecies of the ancient world
concerned King Croesus, shown here in a painting
made in seventeenth-century France.

Is It True?

One afternoon about twenty-five hundred years ago, the stone floor of a temple in Greece disappeared beneath a flood of riches. Under the eyes of the temple priests, messengers unwrapped a glittering treasure: a lion made of gold, enormous gold and silver bowls, barrels of silver, a hundred and seventeen gold bars, and precious necklaces that had belonged to the queen of Lydia, a kingdom in what is now Turkey.

Croesus, the wealthy king of Lydia, had sent this magnificent offering to the temple of Apollo at Delphi, a religious sanctuary on the southern slope of Mount Parnassus in Greece. Why such royal generosity? Because the king wanted something from Delphi. He wanted to know the future.

The temple at Delphi was known far and wide for its oracle, a priestess who answered questions, gave advice, and delivered prophecies— predictions of what was to come. She was called the Pythia. Over the centuries, many different women served as the Pythia, but always they were believed to speak with the voice of Apollo, the god of light and knowledge. Croesus had a vitally important question for the Pythia, and he was sure that she could answer it correctly, because he had come up with a clever way of testing oracular powers.

The king had been comparison shopping for prophecy. Months earlier, he had sent messengers from his capital, Sardis, to seven of the best-known oracles of his time. One messenger went to Delphi. Two messengers went to other temples of Apollo—at Abae, near Delphi, and at Didyma, on the Aegean Sea.

The king's fourth messenger went to Dodona, in the mountains of north-western Greece. There priests and priestesses interpreted the word of Zeus, father of the gods, in the rustling sounds of the leaves in a grove of sacred oak trees. The fifth messenger went south to an oasis in the Libyan Desert of North Africa, where priestesses of the ancient Egyptian god Amon issued prophecies. The sixth messenger went to Oropus, a busy and popular oracle site north of the Greek city of Athens. Oropus was home to Amphiarus, called the son of Apollo. Amphiarus saw the future in his dreams—even, some said, a dream that foretold his own death.

Centuries after the oracles of the ancient world fell silent, Michelangelo painted a priestess of Apollo on the ceiling of Rome's Sistine Chapel.

Croesus's seventh and last messenger went to one of the ancient world's most foreboding oracles: Lebadea, also called Levadia, just twenty miles from Delphi. Another son of Apollo, this one called Trophonius, was believed to have died in a cave there after murdering his brother. In later years, worshippers of Trophonius made the cave into an oracle site. According to Pausanias, a Greek traveler and writer who visited the site almost eight centuries after the time of Croesus, a prophecy in the ominous cave of Trophonius was an eerie event. When Pausanias consulted the oracle, he was told to climb down a ladder into a cavern in the earth. At the bottom he was roughly pulled through a cleft in the rock into a dark chamber, where an unseen speaker answered his question. The experience, Pausanias reported, left some clients "paralyzed with terror."

Each of Croesus's messengers was given a hundred days to reach his destination. Then, on the hundredth day, each messenger asked his oracle the same question: "What is the king of Lydia doing right now?"

The messengers took the seven answers back to Sardis. After reading them, Croesus announced that the Pythia of Delphi had given the most accurate answer (Amphiarus came second). Six of the replies have been lost, but the Greek historian Herodotus later wrote down what the Delphic Pythia said:

I count the grains of sand on the beach and measure the sea; I understand the speech of the dumb and hear the voiceless. The smell has come to my sense of a hard-shelled tortoise boiling and bubbling with lamb's flesh in a bronze pot: The cauldron beneath is of bronze, and of bronze the lid.

As far as modern historians know, lamb-and-turtle stew was not a particular delicacy of the Greeks or Lydians in the middle of the sixth century BCE.* And kings didn't do their own cooking. So an oracle who was simply taking a random stab at guessing the answer to Croesus's question would probably not have said, "Making lamb-and-turtle stew." But according to Herodotus and other ancient writers, the king was doing just that, and in a bronze pot, too.

---

*A variety of systems of dating have been used by different cultures throughout history. Many historians now prefer to use BCE (Before Common Era) and CE (Common Era) instead of BC (Before Christ) and AD (Anno Domini), out of respect for the diversity of the world's peoples.

Croesus was tremendously impressed with the Pythia's accuracy. He sent more messengers to Delphi—this was the group that brought the valuable gifts. These messengers brought another question. It was the question that Croesus had really wanted answered all along, and it concerned war with Persia.

The Persian Empire was based in what is now Iran. It was powerful and much larger than Lydia, with a huge, highly trained army. Its emperor, Cyrus the Great, was determined to enlarge his realm. He was already nibbling at the border of Lydia. How, Croesus wondered, could he protect his kingdom? Maybe a bold, head-on attack would be best. So, after identifying the world's best oracle, the king sent his messengers to ask her this question: Should Croesus invade Persia?

The Pythia replied that if Croesus marched on Persia, he would destroy a mighty empire. Thrilled with this answer, Croesus sent even more gold to Delphi. He then readied his army and ordered it forth to attack the Persians. The king was confident. After all, hadn't the oracle at Delphi foretold his victory?

When the two armies met, the Persians crushed the Lydians. People were amazed and horrified that the oracle had misled Croesus. But the priests at Delphi explained that the prophecy had been accurate. The king had simply failed to interpret it correctly. Croesus's attack on Persia had indeed destroyed a great empire—his own.

Looking Ahead?

Who wouldn't want to catch a glimpse of what lies ahead? Predictions are a fascinating kind of time travel. While most of us know only the past and the present moment, prophets seem to look ahead. Their predictions are like news reports from the unknown future. Sometimes prophets describe a glorious future of peace, progress, and good fortune. A majority of predictions, though,

For the Greek philosopher Plato, there *was* such a thing as sane, or rational, prophecy.

are dire warnings of grievous events: the sinking of the *Titanic*, the assassination of President John F. Kennedy, the end of the world.

The desire to know what is going to happen must be universal. People have been foretelling the future, in one way or another, since the beginning of recorded history (and our prehistoric ancestors probably did it, too).

In the fourth century BCE, the Greek philosopher Plato divided the act of prophesying, or foretelling, into two forms. He called them sane prophecy and insane prophecy. Sane prophecy was an organized, systematic activity in which fortune-tellers interpreted signs whose meanings could be decoded to reveal hidden knowledge about the future. People have used a vast variety of things as signs, from the movements of the planets to the cracks in a burned bone. The questions asked have been just as varied. The oldest known records of fortune-telling reveal such queries as, "Who should inherit my kingdom?" and "When will be the best time for our village to harvest the crops?"

Insane prophecy, or "divine madness," happened when men or women were inspired by gods or spirits, whose otherworldly knowledge was believed to reach into the future. Such prophets revealed "hidden" truths or uttered warnings of what was to come. Sometimes they saw the future in dreams. At other times they spoke under the influence of drugs or alcohol, or during unusual states of mind, such as religious frenzy or trances brought on by music and dancing. Their prophecies could be mysterious and hard to understand. Many were like the Delphic oracle's answer to King Croesus—they were understood only *after* the events they predicted had come to pass.

The Pythia's advice to Croesus may be the world's most famous prediction, or at least the one that is most often quoted. Like many

Reading the future in the entrails of an ox

prophecies, it is ambiguous, which means that it can be interpreted or understood in more than one way. A prophecy that can mean many different things is very difficult to disprove, or to prove, as skeptics have pointed out over the centuries.

A skeptic is someone who requires firm proof to back up claims of things that are extraordinary, such as the ability to see the future. Skeptics are doubtful or critical of claims that are not supported by evidence, or that cannot be tested. From the skeptical point of view, many so-called prophecies don't stand up to close examination. Take the Pythia's words to Croesus—they're not exactly a prophecy. They're more like a statement of fact. When two kingdoms go to war, one is likely to be destroyed. Anyone might have made that prediction, with no special mystical knowledge required. And the prediction would have come true no matter which side won the war.

Putting Prophecy to the Test

If you want to examine a prophecy, the story of Croesus gives you a couple of useful questions to ask. First, is the prophecy ambiguous—could it mean several different things? Or is it so vague and general that it might mean almost anything? Second, is it really a prediction? Or is it the kind of statement that anyone might make, with a little thought?

Take the case of the Seer of Brahan, who lived in the Highlands of Scotland in the seventeenth century CE. The Scots believed that some people possessed "second sight," the ability to see hidden things or foretell the future. Coinneach Odhar (or Kenneth Mackenzie, in English), a farmhand who worked at Brahan Castle, had the gift of prophecy—and died for it, killed in a barrel of boiling tar for being a witch.

Did a seventeenth-century prophet look into the future and foresee the building of this canal? Or are the stories about Coinneach Odhar more fiction than fact?

One of Odhar's prophecies was that someday "full-rigged ships will go east east and west by the back of Tomnahurich Hill." The hill is near Inverness, Scotland. In Odhar's time it was surrounded by dry land. Today the Caledonian Canal, which crosses northern Scotland, runs near the hill. Ships pass through it every day, although now they travel under engine power, not full-rigged sails.

Did Odhar have a vision of the future, or did he simply have a practical idea? The stretch of canal near Inverness is short. It connects two long natural bodies of water that existed in Odhar's day. Canals were known at that time—there were already a few small ones in the British Isles. It might not have needed special powers to think that someday people would build a canal at Inverness.

Prophecy can be hard to prove. Ancient prophecies, like those of the Pythia, were usually written down years or even centuries after they were supposed to have happened. There's no way to be sure people didn't make them up, or change them to make them more interesting. The same is true of many more recent prophets, including the Seer of Brahan. Nothing about Odhar's life or predictions was written down until long after his death. We don't know what he really said, or what has been added to his legend over the years by creative storytellers. Prophecies like his are anecdotes, stories without supporting evidence. But what kind of evidence *could* support a claim about predicting the future?

If someone made a public prediction that was witnessed and recorded in a reliable way, or wrote down a detailed prediction that could later be checked for accuracy, those things could prove the person's ability to see the future (if the predictions came true, of course!). But even with written or public predictions, questions can arise. What are the original sources of information about the prediction—newspaper articles, letters, diary entries? Are they still available for examination, or has the tale of the prediction simply been repeated time after time without anyone checking the facts?

Most important, how many witnesses recorded the prediction, and when? History is full of stories about people who claimed that they had a feeling that something was going to happen, or made a prediction, or heard someone else make one—but they didn't mention it or write it down until *after* the event happened. This doesn't mean that they lied about the feeling or the prediction. But there's no solid proof of it.

Fate, Free Will, and the Future

Once, prophecy was taken very seriously in most parts of the world. In some places, it still is. Even in the industrialized West there are plenty of people who think it is possible to peer into the future. Others share the general scientific view that foretelling the future is impossible, or at least has never been proven. Skeptics say that if people make enough predictions, some of them are bound to be right, simply by chance. There are many more inaccurate predictions than accurate ones, but people tend to remember the "hits" and forget the "misses," so the accurate ones stick out.

Chance, lucky guesses, and common sense surely account for some of the "hits" in the history of prophecy. But do those explanations cover *all* predictions? Maybe people really do catch occasional glimpses of the future. Are such glimpses links to a supernatural realm or a mystical power, as the ancient worshippers at Delphi believed? Some modern believers in prophecy have a different idea. They think it could be the working of a natural force that science does not yet understand. Perhaps it draws on an unknown form of energy or mental activity.

Set aside for a minute the question of whether prophecy is real. Instead, ask yourself what it means to say that people can see into the future. It must mean that the future already exists in some form, otherwise there would be nothing to "see." Imagine yourself on the edge of making a decision—say, choosing between a sandwich and a piece of pizza for lunch. Do you think that your choice is already set and is out there somewhere in "the future," or do you think that you create the future at the moment you make the choice? If you reach for the sandwich but change your mind at the last second, does the future change when you pick up the pizza instead? Or were you always fated to choose pizza, no matter what?

For thousands of years, the world's great thinkers have puzzled over questions like these (not always involving pizza). They have debated whether the future is already set, whether fate or free will

controls our actions. And what about prophecy? If we can know the future, can we change it? No one can answer those questions with certainty, because no one knows what the future is, or even *if* it is. If you have read *Harry Potter and the Half-Blood Prince*, you know that even fiction's most famous boy wizard can't untangle the mysteries of the Hall of Prophecy.

In the pages that follow, you'll explore the many ways people have tried to see the future. You'll find uncannily accurate prophecies and spectacularly bad predictions. You'll also learn more about the Pythia, including some surprising new discoveries about her powers, so that you can form your own ideas about that famous fortune-teller of the ancient world, the Delphic oracle.

The prophet Samuel prepares holy oil for anointing
Saul as king of the Israelites. The Old Testament of the
Bible tells of prophets who did not simply see the
future but also spoke God's word to the people.

Prophets, Oracles, Sibyls, and Seers

Prophesying did not always mean foreseeing the future. Originally it meant revealing any hidden knowledge. That knowledge could be a prediction about the future, but it could also be a vision of something happening far away in the present, as when the Delphic oracle saw King Croesus making stew. To speak any knowledge that wasn't available to ordinary people was to make a prophecy. But because many prophecies were predictions and warnings of things to come, prophecy came to be identified with foretelling the future.

Biblical Prophecy

Prophecy is a key part of many religious traditions. Both Judaism and Christianity recognize prophets, whose visions are described in the Bible. These prophets were considered messengers who heard God's words and spoke them to God's people. In the same way, Muhammad is the prophet of Islam not because he predicted the future but because he communicated the word of God to the Muslim people. The word *divination*, which means "fortune-telling," reminds us that people saw prophecy as a link with the divine.

According to the Bible, there was a right way to prophesy and a wrong way. The Old Testament has examples of both. The right kind of prophets were men of Yahweh, or God. After God revealed things to the prophets in dreams, visions, or trances, the prophets told God's people, the Israelites, what they had learned, even though the people sometimes ignored or scorned their prophetic words.

The first book of Samuel has several descriptions of prophets and prophecy. Samuel was a prophet who knew that a man named Saul was destined to become king of the Israelites. Samuel foretold that Saul would gain the gift of prophecy, too. Samuel instructed Saul to go to a town, "and as you come to the town you will meet a group of prophets coming down from the high place, headed by harp, tambourine, flute, and lyre; they will be in an ecstasy. Then the spirit of Yahweh will seize on you, and you will go into an ecstasy with them, and be changed into another man" (1 Samuel 10:5–8).

The same book tells us that although the ancient Israelites honored divine prophecy, other kinds of foretelling were sinful. Especially wicked were the necromancers—witches or wizards who conjured up the spirits of the dead to learn from them the secrets of the future. Saul banished necromancers from his kingdom—but then, in desperation, he himself turned to this outlawed form of divination.

When a huge enemy army camped in his country, Saul grew afraid. He sought Yahweh's advice but got no answer "either by dream or oracle or prophet." So he asked his servants to find him a necromancer. They sent him to a place called Endor, where a woman practiced the forbidden art of necromancy.

"Disclose the future to me by means of a ghost," Saul told her.

The woman summoned up the spirit of the now-dead prophet Samuel. The prophet was angry at having his rest disturbed, but he delivered a prophecy to Saul—one that terrified the king. Samuel predicted that Saul would be defeated in the next day's battle. The king and his sons would join Samuel in the afterlife. When the battle came, enemy soldiers killed Saul's sons and wounded the king. Saul fell on his own sword rather than be slain by the invaders (1 Samuel 28 and 31).

A book of prophecy ends the Bible's New Testament, which tells the story of Jesus Christ. The book is called Revelation and was

Samuel's ghost reveals the future to Saul. The spirit was summoned by the Witch of Endor, who practiced the forbidden art of necromancy.

The Bible ends with the prophecy of "a new heaven and a new earth," when the sea will disappear and a holy city will descend from above.

written late in the first century CE, a time when Christ's followers were persecuted throughout the Roman Empire. Full of vivid, poetic language, Revelation has been interpreted in hundreds of ways over the past two thousand years.

Many modern scholars believe that part of Revelation describes the suffering of the Christians at the hands of Rome's cruel emperor Nero. But the book also contains visions of the end of the world, the ultimate battle of good and evil, and the triumph of the Christian faith. The author of Revelation said that an angel had shown him the visions. The angel's final words were a list of those who would not be allowed into heaven. Among the outcasts were dogs, murderers, liars, and fortune-tellers (Revelation 22:15).

Soothsayers of the Ancient Greeks

Our modern image of the ancient Greeks is a bit one-sided. Textbooks tell us that the Greeks were pioneers of reason and scientific thinking. They were. But they had another side as well. The Greeks believed in prophecy and practiced it in many forms.

The country was full of soothsayers, or fortune-tellers. Many Greeks wouldn't have dreamed of getting married or setting out on a journey without consulting an astrologer to find out the best day for it. Soothsayers advised people at all levels of society, from generals planning a military campaign to peasants deciding where to put a pigsty.

The oracles and seers, the prophets whose visions came from the gods, held a special place of respect. The most honored of these was the Pythia of Delphi. In his 2006 book *The Oracle: The Lost Secrets and Hidden Message of Ancient Delphi*, science writer William J. Broad describes how important she was to Greek society:

No seer or diviner stood higher. No voice, civil or religious, carried further. No authority was more sought after or more influential. None. She quite literally had the power to depose kings.

The Delphic oracle's power and influence lasted for more than a thousand years. During this long span, the Pythia made a great many prophecies. About six hundred of them are known today. Many are ambiguous, and their meanings remain mysterious. Others deal with the everyday problems of people long dead, so their accuracy cannot be checked.

Some sayings of the Pythia are not really predictions—they are simply answers to questions. For example, during the life of the philosopher Socrates, someone asked the Pythia if a wiser man than Socrates lived. She answered no. (When Socrates heard of this, he said that if he really was wiser than everyone else, it was only because he knew how much he *didn't* know.)

At least one of the Pythia's prophecies probably affected the course of Western history. In 480 BCE, the Persian king Xerxes was ready to invade Greece. The people of Athens feared that their city-state would take the first blow. They sent messengers to the oracle at Delphi to ask whether the gods would protect them. Her answer did not reassure them:

Now your statues are standing
and pouring sweat. They shiver with dread.
The black blood drips from the highest rooftops.
They have seen the necessity of evil. Get out,
get out of my sanctum [inner room] and drown
your spirits in woe!

The Athenians were horrified. Even their statues knew that doom was coming? In despair, they returned to the oracle, humbly asking if she had

The philosopher Socrates was inspired by the Delphic oracle to search for someone wiser than himself.

anything else to tell them. Her answer had three parts. First, the gods would allow "a wall of wood" to remain uncaptured by the Persians. Second, the Athenians should flee from their city. Finally, the island of Salamis, not far from Athens, would "be the death of many a woman's son between the seedtime and the harvest of the grain!"

The oracle's words threw Athens into confusion. Some people thought she was advising them to build wooden walls around part of the city—but why should they flee, if the walls would save them? Others thought that the "wall of wood" was the fleet of Athenian warships, made of wood—but were Greek sailors and soldiers doomed to die at Salamis if they fought the Persians in a naval battle?

Finally, an Athenian leader named Themistocles convinced the people to prepare for a battle at sea. The oracle had said that many *men* would die at Salamis, not necessarily many Greeks. This might mean that the Persians would be defeated there. Then the oracle delivered a new prophecy. The wind, she said, would be the friend of the Greeks. Everyone should pray for wind.

Storms blew up, wrecking part of the Persian fleet and halting a Persian army that was marching on Delphi. The oracle was saved, but the army turned toward Athens. The people abandoned their homes and fled to Salamis, watching from afar as the Persians looted their city and set it afire. The Greek fleet of about three hundred ships moved to Salamis, hoping to protect the island from the Persians' six hundred ships. Then, acting on a plan by Themistocles, the Greeks sailed into a narrow channel between the island and the mainland. When the Persians followed them into the channel, their ships were trapped, without room to move or turn around. The Greek vessels rammed the Persian ones, killing many Persians. After this defeat, Xerxes retreated. The oracle

Greek warriors defeated an invading Persian fleet at the Battle of Salamis, which some believed had been foreseen by the oracle at Delphi. Military historians consider the battle one of history's key turning points.

had pointed the way to a Greek victory—with a little help from Themistocles, who had spent years building up the Athenian war fleet.

A DIVINE MADNESS

Ancient writings give many details about how the oracle at Delphi operated. The Pythia was always a woman from the local community. She was attended—or managed, as some scholars see it—by a group of male priests, who ran the temple. The Pythia prophesied during nine months of the year (Apollo was believed to go elsewhere during the winter), usually only on one day each month. First she performed a ritual that including bathing in a sacred spring. Upon entering the temple, she went to a special chamber in the basement. This chamber was called the *adyton*.

Only the Pythia and the priests could enter the *adyton*. It contained a three-legged stand called a tripod. Beneath the tripod was a natural chasm or crack in the rocky floor. The chasm was the source of the oracle's "divine madness." A mist or vapor that the Greeks called pneuma ("spirit" or "breath") wafted up from the chasm. According to the Greeks, the pneuma came from the rotting carcass of a dragon or giant snake that Apollo had killed and thrown into the chasm, yet it had a pleasant, sweet smell. Once in a while people outside the *adyton* got a whiff of it and became giddy or intoxicated.

Seated on the tripod, holding branches of the laurel tree that was sacred to Apollo, the Pythia breathed the pneuma and passed into mystical union with the god. She could appear drunk, drowsy, or even insane. In this state she uttered her prophecies. Often they made little or no sense, but the priests interpreted them, figuring out her meaning and writing it down. Later, when the Pythia was taken out of the *adyton*, she usually remembered nothing of what Apollo had said with her voice.

Pilgrims seeking advice or prophecy from the Pythia had to go through a ritual, too. They had to travel to Delphi, or send representatives. (All female petitioners had to send male representatives, because only men were allowed to enter the temple.) At Delphi the priests would throw lots like dice. This let chance or the gods decide the order in which pilgrims would get to ask their

Seated on her tripod, holding a sprig of Apollo's sacred laurel, the Pythia enters a visionary state.

questions, although important visitors were sometimes bumped to the head of the line.

A pilgrim was expected to offer a gift to the temple before the prophecy. Many individuals and cities sent gifts afterward, too. Eventually the temple grounds were dotted with treasuries. Prophecy was a solemn religious rite, but it was also big business.

After making his offering, the pilgrim witnessed the sacrifice of a goat. If the sacrifice did not go well—if, for example, the goat did not tremble properly—the prophecy session would not take place. If it did go well, the pilgrim was led down into the temple basement, to a waiting room outside the *adyton*. He could ask one question. Scholars think that the question was passed to the Pythia by the priests. They then gave her answer to the pilgrim and took him back to the surface.

Kings and emperors sought the Pythia's advice. One of them was

The temple of Apollo at Delphi as it might have looked in its heyday, when the oracle wielded great power and influence throughout Greece and beyond.

Alexander the Great, who visited Delphi after conquering Greece. When he learned that he had come at the wrong time, and that the oracle would make no prophecies that day, he stormed into her room and pulled her out. Supposedly she exclaimed, "This young man is unstoppable!" Alexander took her words for a prophecy that he would succeed in his plan to conquer western Asia—which he did.

A few centuries later the Roman emperor Nero, who had murdered his mother, came to Delphi. The Pythia told him, "Begone, mother-killer! Your presence outrages me!" Furious at what he considered an insult from the oracle, Nero had the priests tortured and then buried alive with the Pythia. But the temple recovered, and a new Pythia mounted the tripod. A few years later a young Roman pilgrim named Hadrian learned at Delphi that he would become emperor someday. When he came to the throne in 117 CE, he ordered the temple closed so that no other ambitious young man would be encouraged to see himself as a future emperor.

By that time, the oracle at Delphi had already lost some of its importance in the ancient world. Soon the rising power of Christianity would finish it off. The church believed that the oracle's ability to prophesy was real, but not divine. All non-Christian oracles, according to the Christian writers and bishops, were the work of the devil. When the Roman Empire officially became Christian in the early fourth century, the remaining pagan shrines were shut down.

Delphi had a final, brief moment of glory when a young man named Julian became the emperor of Rome in 361. Julian tried to bring back the worship of the pre-Christian gods. He hoped to restore the Delphic oracle to importance and promised to protect the priests and the Pythia if they reopened the temple. The last oracle sent Julian this message: "Bright Apollo no longer has a roof over his head, a prophetic laurel or a babbling spring. Yes, even the murmuring water has dried up." The Pythia's final prophecy was accurate. The days of the Delphic oracle were over. Julian, who ruled for just two years, failed to halt the advance of Christianity.

THE CUMAEAN SIBYL

One ancient prophet did receive some respect from the church. She was the Cumaean Sibyl, Rome's answer to the Delphic oracle. According to Greek and Roman myths, Sibylla was a prophetess in the distant past, at the time of the Trojan War. Because of her, some female prophets were called sibyls. One of them lived in a cave at Cumae, in Italy. She wrote the answers to pilgrims' questions on the leaves of palm trees. Roman legends

Legend says that the Cumaean Sibyl carried her books of prophecy to Rome, where she sold them to King Tarquinius at a high price.

said that in the sixth century BCE a Roman king named Tarquinius bought three books of prophecy from the Cumaean Sibyl. The sibylline books were stored in a temple in Rome. Whenever the city faced danger, its leaders would look in the books for advice.

The sibylline books eventually disappeared, perhaps in a fire or barbarian invasion, but a few prophecies were remembered. When Christians later read them, they thought that the Sibyl had predicted Christ's birth. For this reason, church authorities considered the Cumaean Sibyl much more respectable than the other pagan prophets. Her image even appears in Christian artwork.

Native American Prophets and Oracles

The people who lived in the Americas before the Europeans arrived had their own traditions of prophecy. Healers and visionaries communicated wisdom and predictions from the spirit world, sometimes after dreams or trances. Such healers are sometimes called shamans, and they are found in many cultures around the globe.

In North America, the Indians fought a centuries-long battle against the white Europeans and Americans who destroyed their traditional cultures and drove them from their lands. Out of this struggle arose many Indian prophets, claiming to be guided by the spirits. They described visions of victory over the whites and a return to the old Indian ways. Often, these prophets provided inspiration for acts of resistance and revolt.

One of the most influential Indian visionaries was Tenskwatawa, the brother of the Shawnee chieftain Tecumseh. He had studied healing under a shaman. Then, around 1805, he started having visions. In these visions, a great spirit called the Master of Life instructed him on how the Indians should live if they wished to triumph over the Americans, who were moving into Shawnee territory

A nineteenth-century Native American shaman holds a sacred rattle and stirs a medicinal potion. Shamans often claimed prophetic powers.

in the Ohio River valley. The Indians, said the Master of Life, should abandon all of the white man's goods, including alcohol and guns (although they could use guns against the settlers). They should live together in peace, and follow their old beliefs and customs.

Tenskwatawa came to be known as the Shawnee Prophet. He attracted followers to a settlement in northeastern Indiana. The whites called it Prophetstown. In 1811 U.S. Army troops marched on Prophetstown while Tecumseh, the war leader, was away. Tenskwatawa told his followers that they should attack the soldiers, whose bullets would not hurt them. His prediction was fatally wrong, and Prophetstown was destroyed. Although the Shawnee Prophet survived the attack, his hold on the Indians was broken.

Centuries earlier, before the Europeans came, a Native American oracle site called Pachacamac was as famous in Peru as Delphi was in Greece. The temple there was a 500-foot (150-meter) pyramid of sunbaked brick. A series of Peruvian peoples believed it was the home of Pachacamac, their creator god. For a thousand years or so, pilgrims came to receive the wisdom of Pachacamac, communicated by the temple priests.

The oracle at Pachacamac came to a sudden end in 1533 at the hands of the Spanish conquistadores who invaded Peru. They searched the temple for treasure and shut down the oracle. Thanks to Atahualpa, the last emperor of Peru's Inca people, we know Pachacamac's final prophecy. The oracle predicted that Atahualpa would kill all of the Spanish invaders. The oracle, as Atahualpa bitterly told the conquistadores who had captured him and would later kill him, was wrong.

Another prophecy from the ancient Americas survives in the form of a calendar. The Maya, who lived in southern Mexico and part of Central America, developed an elaborate calendar system and used it for divination. Each day in the calendar was governed by astrological and religious signs. Diviners read these signs to know whether a day was lucky or unlucky for certain activities.

The Maya measured time in units. The biggest unit was the Long Count, which measured an entire cycle of the world's existence. Modern scholars who have studied the Maya calendar believe that the Long Count started on August 11, 3114 BCE. The last day of the Long Count will be December 21, 2012. The Maya believed that the world as we know it will end on that day.

Was the prediction contained in the Maya calendar true? If you're reading this sentence on or after December 22, 2012, you know the answer.

Can this chunk of cheese reveal the future?
The medieval practice of tiromancy, or reading
the future in the patterns formed during
cheese making, is a lost art today.

2

Reading the Signs

I s secret knowledge hidden in the world around us? People in almost every culture have thought so. At one time or another, soothsayers have tried to read the future, the will of the gods, and the answers to their questions in all kinds of things—from tea leaves to tarot cards to the scuttling of a spider.

In some cultures, only specialists were skilled in the art of reading these signs. Such people might serve the community as priests, professional diviners, or both. In other places, though, the art of divination was widely known, and ordinary people used the tools of prediction. The relationship between religion and fortune-telling has also varied from place to place and time to time. Divination has been honored by some governments and churches but forbidden by others.

Today many kinds of fortune-telling have fallen out of fashion. Few people are likely to practice the medieval art of tiromancy—cheese reading—in which the pattern of holes in cheese tells the future. But other old forms of divination, such as astrology, remain as popular as ever.

Omens, Augurs, and Auspices

Hundreds of systems of divination, maybe thousands, have existed. They fall into two broad groups. One kind of divination reads signs that occur naturally, such as the movements of planets, the flights of birds, or the weather. In the other form of divination, the diviner (or the person who is asking the question) takes an active role, perhaps by dealing a deck of cards, throwing a pair of sticks, or placing a bone or a tortoise shell in a fire so that heat will cause a pattern of cracks that can be interpreted.

Signs in the natural world are sometimes called omens. Perhaps no society has paid more attention to omens than the ancient Romans. They even established an official bureau of omen-reading soothsayers called augurs, who practiced augury.

Eruptions of Mount Vesuvius really were bad omens for ancient Rome. The volcano buried whole towns.

Roman augury was the kind of fortune-telling that the Greeks had called "sane prophecy." It wasn't meant to reveal the future in the way that the inspired prophecies of oracles did. Instead, it was supposed to give matter-of-fact advice to individuals and the state. Augurs told whether the gods approved or disapproved of people's plans and actions. Roman leaders always consulted augurs before making important decisions, or when a crisis appeared.

One form of Roman augury involved dividing the sky into sixteen sections, each of which was governed by a god. If a bird flew through that section of sky, or a bolt of lightning flashed in it, or clouds moved across it, the augur interpreted the omen as a sign of the god's will. Omens were either auspicious (good) or inauspicious (bad). When the omens were inauspicious, the prudent Roman waited for a better day. The verdict of the state augurs could postpone public events ranging from festivals to wars.

Prodigies were another kind of omen that the Romans took very seriously. A prodigy was anything remarkable, unusual, or disastrous. The eruption of a volcano was a prodigy. So was the birth of a deformed person or animal. These disturbing events meant that the gods were displeased. To mend their relationship with the gods, or to seek clearer answers than the omens could provide, the Romans sought the advice of a special kind of diviner called a haruspex.

Haruspices existed everywhere in the ancient world. Some scholars think that their particular art, called haruspicy or extispicy, may be the oldest known form of divination. It involved the ritual sacrifice of animals—or, in rare cases, human beings.

The sacrifical victim was cut open, and the haruspex read the omens in the shape of its entrails (its insides), especially the intestines and the liver. The haruspices of Mesopotamia, in what is now Iraq, had a highly developed system of entrail reading. They divided the liver into fifty-five sections and studied the shape, color, and markings of each section.

The Incas of South America practiced extispicy, too. Their sacrificial animal was a white llama. Priests blew into the dead animal's lungs, studied the shapes made by the veins on the surface of the lungs, and interpreted

A Mesopotamian model of a sheep's liver tells haruspices how to interpret the signs.

those shapes as guides to action. Today, traditional healers among the Peruvian Indians still perform extispicy, but now they use black guinea pigs. When a person is sick, a shaman performs a ceremony that is supposed to give the person's illness to the guinea pig. The shaman then kills the animal and examines its entrails for information about the illness. Similar kinds of fortune-telling by extispicy occur in Africa, Asia, and Latin America.

Some divination involving animals is less gruesome. The Romans favored a system still used today in parts of the world—chicken divination. They scattered grains of wheat in a pattern that represented various auspicious and inauspicious meanings. Then they waited to see which grains the chicken picked up. Roman armies on the march carried chickens for this purpose.

In the West African nation of Cameroon, soothsayers of the Mambila people use spiders for divination. They place dried leaves marked

A rooster and a hen from an ancient Roman wall painting. The Romans used such fowl in a form of divination still practiced today.

with symbols near the burrows of large, ground-dwelling spiders and wait to see which leaves the spiders move. This kind of divination is taken so seriously that in recent years people have been convicted of sorcery and sent to prison as witches on the word of spider diviners.

Sortilege, or casting lots, is mentioned in the Bible and many other ancient sources. People around the world still use sortilege to answer questions. The questioner tosses two or more small objects, such as pebbles, bones, sticks, dice, shells, or nuts. The answer lies in the way they fall. Depending upon the system being used, the answer may be a simple yes or no, or it may require detailed interpretation.

Warriors cast lots in a scene on a Greek vase made in the sixth century BCE.

One of the oldest systems of sortilege is found in a Chinese book called the *I Ching*. The method involves throwing coins or plant stalks. The results of the throws make up symbols called hexagrams. There are sixty-four possible hexagrams, and the book gives an interpretation of each one. The interpretations are somewhat vague and ambiguous—in fact, most of them can be read not just in different ways but in opposite ways. Yet many people who use the *I Ching* don't turn to it for predictions. Instead, they seek new ways of thinking about their problems. Carl Jung, one of the founders of modern psychology, thought that the *I Ching* was a valuable tool for tapping into inner knowledge.

Heavens Above

Have you ever read your horoscope in a magazine or online? If so, you've taken part in astrology, one of the world's oldest forms of divination. Astrology is based on the idea that the positions and movements of the heavenly bodies, especially the planets, are connected with life on earth. Astrologers have used the heavens to forecast events, give advice, and describe people's personalities and their outlook for good or bad fortune.

Thousands of years ago, stargazers in many parts of the world began recording the movements of the heavenly bodies. From these observations came calendars for measuring months and years. People also started to make connections between what they saw in the heavens and what happened on earth, and astrology was born.

Astrology has taken many forms. Chinese astrology is based on the phases of the moon and also on a sixty-year cycle. Days and years are identified with animals, colors, and elements. These things in turn symbolize characteristics, such as strength, or events, such as a journey or a death. The astrologer produces a horoscope that shows the person's relationship to the meaningful animals, colors, and elements.

Most Western systems of astrology come from methods developed in ancient Mesopotamia and Egypt. In these systems, the part of the sky through which the planets move is called the zodiac. It is divided into twelve regions, and a star constellation is the symbol, or sign, for each region. A horoscope is based on the positions of the moon and planets in these signs of the zodiac at the time of a person's birth.

The simplest horoscopes use only the sun's place on the day

The twelve signs of the zodiac form the basis of Western astrology.

of birth. These "sun sign" horoscopes are the ones you find in newspapers and magazines, listed under the twelve astrological signs. They aren't very personal—after all, the prediction for each sign is supposed to cover a twelfth of the world's population! Many serious astrologers consider sun-sign horoscopes all but worthless.

Full horoscopes are based on the date, time, and place of birth. These charts, sometimes called natal horoscopes, are the most common kind of horoscope in the West. People in Asia also use natal charts. In addition, they consult horary charts, which are based on the position of the heavenly bodies at the time a question is asked. These charts tell people whether or not to do something at a particular time. A mundane horoscope deals with astrological events that are believed to affect large groups of people, or even the whole world, such as when two or three planets appear close together in the sky.

The zodiacal man represents the zodiac in human form.

The history of astrology is full of ups and downs. Like other forms of divination, it was respected and widely used throughout most of the ancient world. Astrology faded somewhat in western Europe after about the sixth century CE, partly because people had forgotten the old Greek and Roman astrological books and partly because the Christian church frowned on it. Then, starting around the twelfth century, astrology gained new strength.

Today we see a difference between astronomy, the scientific study of the heavens, and astrology, divination based on the heavens. In Europe five or six centuries ago, astrology *was* the science. Scholars and stargazers devoted much energy to it. Royalty and church officials turned to learned astrologers for guidance. Advice from the stars was considered essential to any risky venture.

Ferdinand Magellan, who discovered the sea route around South America in the early sixteenth century, took an astrologer named Andres de San Martín on his perilous voyage. When one of the ships in Magellan's fleet went missing, the explorer asked San Martín what had happened to it. The astrologer said that an officer named Gomes had mutinied, seized the ship, and headed back to Spain. Years later, when the survivors of the expedition returned to Europe, they learned that that was exactly what had happened.

Portuguese explorer Ferdinand Magellan had an astrologer on his around-the-world voyage— but got no warning of his own death.

Believers in astrology point to the story of Magellan's missing ship as proof that astrology works. But could there be another explanation? A report of the voyage written by an Italian member of the expedition shows that Gomes had long been a complainer and troublemaker. Magellan had already crushed one mutiny, and there were signs that another could break out at any moment. So San Martín's answer might have been based on common sense as much as on the stars.

Many astrologers seem to have been good observers of human nature and behavior as well as of the heavens.

Astrologers could also be shrewd thinkers. One story about Louis XI, king of France in the fifteenth century, says that he was angry at his astrologer and threatened to have the man executed. The astrologer offered a final prediction. "I shall die three days before your majesty," he said. The king called off the execution.

An Italian astrologer named Girolamo Cardano died for divination in 1576. Cardano was a perfect example of the man of learning whose interests included astrology. He was a mathematician and a doctor and

Louis XI at prayer. The king of France spared the life of his quick-thinking astrologer.

teacher of medicine who made horoscopes for important people, including King Edward VI of England. But in 1570 Cardano went too far. He claimed to have cast the horoscope of Jesus Christ. The church considered this a crime and threw Cardano into prison. He cast his own horoscope, predicting the date and time of his death. When that time came, some historians say, Cardano killed himself so that his prediction would be accurate.

By Cardano's time, astrology was entering a difficult era. Astronomy was emerging as a science shaped by new discoveries that changed our knowledge of the heavens. The age-old belief that the earth was the center of the universe was shattered. Instead of revolving around the earth, as astrologers had always thought, the planets (including the earth) revolve around the sun. Eventually, the discovery of new planets seemed to deal a fatal blow to astrology. How reliable could an ancient system of reading the planets possibly be, when it hadn't even known that planets such as Uranus and Neptune existed?

Yet the twentieth century brought a surge of new interest and passionate belief in astrology. Some people today are drawn to astrology because they mistrust science, or because the scientific view of the world doesn't fulfill their spiritual needs. Others think that astrology *is* a science, based on natural laws that are not yet understood, and that it can be tested and proved. A few researchers have designed ways to test astrology, but no solid proof has yet been shown.

For centuries people debated whether the movements of the heavenly bodies caused earthly events or only revealed them. Today, these questions have been put aside by some astrologers, who prefer to use horoscopes as tools to help people think about their personalities, choices, and goals.

It's in the Cards

Cartomancy is divination using cards. Some methods use ordinary playing cards. Others use special decks. The most famous of these is the tarot. Like the *I Ching* and astrology, the tarot has more than one use. Some people use it for fortune-telling. Others consider it an aid to insight and self-discovery. Although historians have tried to trace the origins of the tarot to the ancient world, there is no evidence of it before the fourteenth century CE. The oldest known decks are from Italy and France, but Europeans may have borrowed an early form of the tarot from the Islamic world.

Originally the tarot had fifty-six cards in four groups, or suits. Later another twenty-two cards were added. Instead of belonging to suits, these new cards were simply given numbers. In time each of these became associated with a symbol, name, and meaning, such as Death, the Lovers, the Hanged Man, and the Wheel of Fortune. The suits are called the minor arcana; the named cards are the major arcana.

One of the easiest methods of divination with the tarot involves choosing ten cards from the major arcana and laying them in a pattern. Positions in the pattern stand for such things as the subject's past, his or her goal, obstacles blocking the goal, and so on.

At first, though, people used the tarot simply for playing card games—the Italian game *tarocco* may be the origin of the word *tarot*. Then, in the late eighteenth century, cartomancy became fashionable in France, and people started laying out patterns of cards to tell fortunes. Before long, they were using the tarot for that purpose. Around that time, several books were published in France and England which invented a false history of the tarot, linking it to the magicians of ancient Egypt.

In recent years, diviners and artists have created countless new versions of the tarot deck. There are decks with Native American themes, scenes from famous paintings, characters from the tales of King Arthur or *The Lord of the Rings*, pictures of animals, Japanese cartoons, dragons, baseballs players, and images from many religions and cultures. The tarot, it seems, has something for everyone, and that may be the secret of its appeal.

Death, stalked by the shadow of the Grim Reaper

Jeane Dixon, photographed around 1960, became one of
the best-known psychics in the United States on the
strength of a famous presidential prediction.

Visions of the Future

On May 13, 1956, *Parade* magazine published a prediction by Jeane Dixon, a Washington, DC, woman who had a reputation for foretelling the future. Someone had asked Dixon who would win the next presidential election.

"As for the 1960 election," the magazine reported, "Mrs. Dixon thinks it will be dominated by labor and won by a Democrat. He will be assassinated in office, 'though not necessarily in his first term.'"

Four years later, Democrat John F. Kennedy was elected president. Three years after that, he was shot to death. Jeane Dixon, who died in 1997, went down in history as "the woman who predicted the Kennedy assassination." The truth is a little more complicated, as it always is.

Dixon said that she started seeing the future when she was eight years old. When she grew up, she and her husband owned a real-estate business in the nation's capital, and she got to know many people in Washington society. By her own account she forecast the future for leading political figures, including Presidents Franklin D. Roosevelt and Harry S. Truman. Later in her career she was rumored to be one of the unofficial White House astrologers to President Ronald Reagan and his wife, Nancy. She said that her prophecies came to her through many means: a crystal ball, astrology, prayer, dreams, psychic power or mind reading, and sudden visions or premonitions.

The Kennedy prediction is Dixon's best-known "hit," or correct prediction. Many people have heard of it. Most of them have not heard of another prediction she made in 1960, before the election. She stated that "John F. Kennedy would fail to win the presidency" and predicted that Richard Nixon, a Republican, would win it. This flatly contradicted Dixon's earlier prophecy that a Democrat would be elected in 1960. But the first prediction, with its dramatic link to the tragic assassination of Kennedy, has been repeated many times in books about prophecy and psychic powers. The second one is usually ignored.

Dixon had other hits. In 1978 she predicted that "a dreadful plague will strike down thousands of people in this country," and a few years later the AIDS virus started claiming many lives. Late in 1988 she predicted that "a shipping accident will make headlines in the spring." The following March the *Exxon Valdez* spilled oil in Alaskan waters. A skeptic might say that these predictions are so loose that they could apply to many different events. Dixon did make other, more specific predictions that came true, such as forecasting the suicide of actress Marilyn Monroe. Some of Dixon's most accurate predictions cannot be proved because they took place in private conversations and were not recorded until much later.

Among Dixon's public predictions, which usually appeared in tabloid newspapers, the misses outnumbered the hits. She predicted that World War III would start in 1958, that the Russians would land a man on the moon before the Americans did, that the Vietnam War would last only ninety days, that the United States would have a woman president in the 1980s, and that a huge comet would strike the earth in that same decade, causing one of the worst natural disasters of the century. Dixon also forecast that by the end of the twentieth century the Roman Catholic Church would disappear and peace would come to the Middle East.

Although none of these predictions came true, people continued to believe in Dixon's prophetic gifts. John Allen Paulos, a mathematician at Temple University in Philadelphia, invented the term "Jeane Dixon effect" to describe the way believers in fortune-telling focus on a small number of hits and never mention the larger number of misses. The Jeane Dixon effect doesn't apply only to modern psychics. It can also color the way people look at history's best-known seers.

Nostradamus

One of the most remarkable prophetic writings ever created is a history of the future in more than 940 poems of four lines each. It was the work of Michel de Nostredame, better known as Nostradamus.

Hundreds of books have been written about Nostradamus and

his prophecies. Scholars, believers, and skeptics debate the meaning of his predictions—or their lack of meaning. But whether or not Nostradamus really predicted the future, he produced a book that, like a huge crossword puzzle or brainteaser, has fascinated thinkers ever since.

Nostradamus lived in the southern French region of Provence in the first half of the sixteenth century. He came

Nostradamus created a long-lasting mystery with his set of puzzling poems that some consider prophecies.

from a Jewish family that had converted to Catholicism to avoid being persecuted. Many of his writings seem to reflect the religious strife that ran high in Europe in his day, with Catholics and Protestants turned against each other and both of them hostile to Jews.

Trained as a doctor, Nostradamus gained fame for treating victims of bubonic plague. Even if he had never become a prophet, Nostradamus would deserve respect for his brave and compassionate work in medicine. His success rate was higher than that of most doctors, perhaps because he recommended sanitary procedures such as washing bedclothes and drinking clean water. His success rate was not perfect, however. He lost his first wife and two children to plague.

In 1547 Nostradamus remarried and settled in the town of Salon. He lived there until his death in 1566, although he traveled in France and possibly in Italy as well. He exchanged letters with many learned scholars of the day and also visited the royal court in Paris, where he gave astrological forecasts to the royal family.

Many stories seem to illustrate Nostradamus's prophetic powers. According to one anecdote that is often repeated, he once visited someone who showed him a white pig and a black one. The host asked Nostradamus to predict which pig they would eat for dinner. Nostradamus said that they would eat the black pig and that a wolf would eat the white one. The host, planning to falsify the prediction, secretly told his cook to prepare the white pig. When the pig was served, Nostradamus claimed it was the black one. The host investigated. He found that his pet wolf cub had eaten the white pig, so the cook had prepared the black one after all.

The trouble with the pig story and many others about Nostradamus is that they weren't written down until many years after the seer's death. In fact, some Nostradamus anecdotes have strong echoes of stories about other seers.

Whatever the truth about the two pigs, by 1550 Nostradamus

The spirit of Nostradamus, who died in 1566, warns King William III of England. Some say the seer foretold the death of the king, which occurred in 1704.

had a reputation as a seer. That year he started publishing annual forecasts of events that would take place during the coming year. Five years later he published the first version of his book. It contained 353 prophetic poems and was called *Centuries*. The title doesn't refer to hundred-year time spans. It comes from the fact that the poems, called quatrains, were grouped into batches of one hundred. Nostradamus published more quatrains three years later. Still more appeared two years after his death. One problem with the study of the *Centuries* is that there were many differences among early printings of the books. Modern scholars do not agree on how many quatrains are authentic, or on their exact wording.

They don't agree on much else about Nostradamus, either. How, for example, did Nostradamus arrive at his insights? One theory is that he used an elaborate astrological system. Another theory, suggested by his own words, is that he sat on a tripod like the Delphic oracle and had trancelike visions.

The interpretation of Nostradamus's quatrains is a challenge for many reasons. First, the Prophet of Provence did not write an orderly history of the future, starting with next year and proceeding to the end of the world. The quatrains are presented in no particular order, and almost none of them contains clues to specific dates. Even the quatrains that *do* contain numbers can be interpreted to give different dates. This means that just about any one of the hundreds of quatrains could apply to any event since Nostradamus's time, or tomorrow, or next year.

Nostradamus's work was published in several forms, making it hard to know what he really wrote.

To make matters even more complicated, Nostradamus delivered his predictions in the form of little puzzles or riddles. They were written in a regional dialect of French, with a generous sprinkling of Greek, Latin, Hebrew, and Arabic terms. He also used puns and words that might be coded symbols. All in all, the quatrains are definitely mysterious! People who cannot read them in their original language risk being misled by one of the many careless or outright fake translations that circulate in books and on the Internet.

After all that, what about the prophecies? Did Nostradamus really see the future?

A handful of the quatrains seem to be dramatic matches with things that happened after they were written. The closest match, and the most famous quatrain, is number 35 of the first century of poems. In English, it reads:

The young lion will overcome the old.
On a field of war in a single [or singular] duel,
In a cage of gold his eyes he will pierce:
Two wounds into one, then he dies a cruel death.

Many people in the sixteenth century and later have believed that this quatrain predicted an event that took place in 1559. King Henry II of France was accidentally killed while jousting with spears in a tournament. His opponent was a nobleman six years younger than

The 1559 tournament during which Henry II of France was killed— an old lion slain by a young one, in the words of Nostradamus

the king. Both men's shields bore lions as emblems. The younger man's spear splintered and pierced the king's barred helmet—there may have been two splinters, and the helmet may have been covered with gold, but these things are not known for certain. The king died a lingering, painful death from a wound to his brain.

Many people think that quatrain 60, also of the first century of poems, predicted the birth of Napoleon Bonaparte and his rise to power in the eighteenth century. It says:

An Emperor will be born near Italy,
Who will cost the Empire dear:
People will say when they see his followers
That he is less a prince than a butcher.

Napoleon was born on the island of Corsica, near Italy. He became emperor of France, and some might call his far-ranging wars a kind of butchery.

Other quatrains have been linked to a host of historical events, including the London fire of 1666; the beheading of Queen Marie Antoinette of France; the death of President Kennedy; the September 11, 2001, terrorist attacks on Washington, DC, and New York City; and many more. Often just one or two lines or phrases appear to fit the events, and the interpreters have had to use a lot of imagination, and some wordplay, to find the matches. Other quatrains remain completely obscure. They may refer to things that haven't happened yet.

Whatever meanings they might hold, Nostradamus's quatrains are not very useful as predictions. No one in 1558, for example, thought that the quatrain about the two lions was a warning of King Henry's death. *After* the king died, people noticed that the quatrain might have foretold it. The same is true of the other revelations that people have seen in his quatrains. So, does Nostradamus have anything to tell us about the future? Maybe. He hinted that his prophecies were accurate to the year 3797. He also mentioned that he'd had visions of the world seven thousand years after his time. He didn't give details—but at least Nostradamians, as his admirers are called, can take comfort in the fact that the world isn't going to end anytime soon.

The End of the World and Other Disasters

Mother Shipton's followers feared that the world was going to end in the late nineteenth century. Ursula Sontheil, called Mother Shipton after her marriage, was an English prophet who lived at about the same time as Nostradamus. Her mother had been accused of being a witch, and Mother Shipton herself was said to have second sight.

During her lifetime, Mother Shipton gained followers called Shiptonists. After she died, in 1561, her predictions were published

in pamphlets and books. By the time Charles Hindley wrote *Life, Prophecies, and Death of the Famous Mother Shipton* in 1862, she really was famous. In the years that followed, people grew agitated about one of her prophecies:

When the world to an end shall come,
in eighteen hundred and eighty one.

As the year 1880 drew to a close, some people in England feared that the

Mother Shipton is called England's Nostradamus, but many of her prophecies were written centuries after her death.

end of the world was at hand. When the world kept going past 1881, they decided that Mother Shipton must have meant "*nineteen* hundred and eighty one." Later, however, Hindley revealed that he had made up that prophecy and others in order to sell more copies of his book.

Yet Mother Shipton is said to have made another prediction about the end of the world, one that isn't tied to a specific date. It says, "The world shall end when the High Bridge is thrice fallen." She was referring to a bridge in her hometown of Knaresborough, Yorkshire. Since her day, the bridge has fallen down and been repaired twice.

Edgar Cayce gained renown as both a healer and a prophet of doom and cataclysm.

Edgar Cayce didn't predict the end of the world, but he foresaw disasters unlike any others in human history. Cayce has been called the American Nostradamus, but he was more often called the Sleeping Prophet because he gave most of his psychic readings and prophecies while in a trance.

Cayce was born in rural Hopkinsville, Kentucky, in 1877. Although he had some hope of becoming a minister, Cayce left school when he was fifteen. By that time, he later said, he had developed psychic abilities, such as being able to learn the contents of books by sleeping with them under his head. Later he turned his gift toward healing.

In time Cayce developed a method that he used both for healing and for giving prophecies. Resting on a couch or bed, he would hypnotize himself into a light trance, a semiconscious state. Then his wife or an assistant would read questions from people seeking advice, and he would answer. Later, after waking up, he would have no recollection of what he had said.

As Cayce's reputation grew, so did the number of letters he received, asking for his psychic help. Most of the questions he answered had to do with sickness. People read newspaper articles about his healing ability and wrote to him from all over the world. He diagnosed their conditions and prescribed treatments, usually without ever seeing his patients. Cayce gave a vast number of readings this way and received a great many reports of cures from grateful patients. Thousands of his readings are stored at the Association for Research and Enlightenment, an institute that Cayce founded in Virginia in 1931.

When it came to predicting the future, Cayce's record was mixed. Several of his statements were timely, specific, and insightful. Six months before the stock market crash of 1929, for example, Cayce advised a friend to sell his stocks, warning him that there would be a crash. Before World War II broke out, he told soldiers to prepare for duty.

Fortunately, Cayce's more alarming predictions have failed to come true. He prophesied that the second half of the twentieth century would bring immense geological upheavals. California would slide into the sea, followed by parts of Europe and Japan. As if to make up for these losses, the legendary continent of Atlantis would rise from the ocean off the eastern coast of the United States. To round off the century, in 1999 thousands of volcanoes all over the planet would erupt, bringing about the fall of civilization. Still, Cayce's predictions are no darker than those of many other prophets who have spoken of natural disasters and great wars to come. And like many of those prophets, Cayce also foresaw civilization rebuilding itself from the wreckage.

This World War I soldier said his premonitions were a
sign of his "special destiny." At the time, no one foretold that
young Adolf Hitler would become a murderous tyrant.

4

Dreams and Premonitions

During World War I, trenches snaked across the battlefields of Europe. Thousands of soldiers spent months in these trenches while their armies bombarded one another. One day a young soldier was eating dinner with his comrades when something strange happened.

"Suddenly a voice seemed to be saying to me, 'Get up and go over there,'" he later reported. "It was so clear and insistent that I obeyed mechanically as if it had been an officer's order. I rose at once to my feet and walked twenty yards along the trench, carrying my dinner in its tin-can. I then sat down to go on eating, my mind once more at rest. Hardly had I done so when a flash and deafening roar came from the part of the trench I had just left. A stray shell had burst over the men where I had been sitting, everyone was killed."

If that soldier's story is true, he had a premonition, an urgent feeling that he should do something. By obeying it, he lived while others died. The same soldier claimed that similar premonitions helped him escape several other brushes with death during World War I. A few decades later, another devastating war was started by that soldier, whose name was Adolf Hitler. In Hitler's view, his amazing escapes during the first war showed that he was a person of special destiny, a leader who was fated to bring Germany back to power.

A Dream of Death

Hitler's premonition in the trench took the form of an immediate order to action. Many other people have claimed to foresee their own deaths, or the deaths of other people, but their foreknowledge did not change the outcome.

President Abraham Lincoln, according to some accounts of his life, believed in the prophetic power of dreams. He also expressed fears that he would come to a tragic end—something that was quite possible during the Civil War, when Southerners hated and threatened the president and he had to travel with bodyguards. One frequent body-guard was a friend named Ward H. Lamon. In April 1865 the president told Lamon about a disturbing dream. Lamon later recounted it:

About ten days ago, I retired very late. I had been up waiting for important dispatches from the front. I could not have been long in bed when I fell into a slumber, for I was weary. I soon began to dream. There seemed to be a death-like stillness about me. Then I heard subdued sobs, as if a number of people were weeping. I thought I left my bed and wandered downstairs. There the silence was broken by the same pitiful sobbing, but the mourners were invisible. I went from room to room; no living person was in sight, but the same mournful sounds of distress met me as I passed along. I saw light in all the rooms; every object was familiar to me; but where were all the people who were grieving as if their hearts would break? I was puzzled and alarmed. What could be the meaning of all this? Determined to find the cause of a state of things so mysterious and so shocking, I kept on until I arrived at the East Room, which I entered. There I met with a sickening surprise. Before me was a cata-falque, on which rested a corpse wrapped in funeral vestments. Around it were stationed soldiers who were acting as guards; and there was a throng of people, gazing mournfully upon the corpse, whose face was covered, others weeping pitifully. "Who is dead in the White House?" I demanded of one of the soldiers. "The President," was his answer; "he was killed by an assassin." Then came a loud burst of grief from the crowd, which woke me from my dream.

According to Lamon, Lincoln had this dream just three days before he was shot and killed by an assassin. Lamon published the story of the dream many years after Lincoln's death.

The literature of prophecy is filled with accounts of dreams that accurately predicted deaths of loved ones or friends. Sometimes the dream warns of the death of a public figure, such as a president or celebrity. An unusually detailed example of this kind of dream comes from Cornwall, England. There, on May 11, 1812, a mining engineer named John Williams dreamed that he was in London, in the government building called the House of Commons. He saw a man in a brown coat shoot a man who was wearing a blue coat and a white vest. Someone said that the man in blue was "the chancellor." Williams woke up and shared the dream with his wife, then went back to sleep—and dreamed it again. The next day his son brought news from London. The chancellor of the exchequer, Britain's treasurer, had been shot and killed in the House of

One of Abraham Lincoln's aides claimed that the president foresaw his own death.

Commons the night before. The victim and his killer had been wearing clothes that matched those in Williams's dream.

The sinking of the luxury liner *Titanic* in April 1912 launched a flood of stories about premonitions. Many people reported that they had canceled plans to sail aboard the ship because they had a feeling of coming disaster, or a dream of a sinking ship. This is not surprising—researchers who study prophecy and prediction know that every major disaster produces a number of similar reports afterward, and the sinking of the *Titanic* was the biggest disaster of its time.

It's impossible to be sure that those who claimed premonitions about the *Titanic* really had them, or spoke of them before the tragedy. But many people think that two works of fiction that were published *before* the ship sank foretold the *Titanic*'s fate.

One story was "From the Old World to the New," published in 1893. Its author, W. J. Stead, was an English journalist and spiritualist who believed in psychic communication with the dead. Stead's story involved a huge liner and its captain, Edward J. Smith. The liner sank in the Atlantic Ocean after colliding with another ship. Many passengers perished because there were not enough lifeboats to save them all. More than twenty years later, in an eerie twist of fate, W. J. Stead's name appeared in the list of passengers who drowned after the *Titanic* hit an iceberg and sank. The captain of the *Titanic* was Edward J. Smith—and his ship lacked enough lifeboats for all its passengers.

Even stranger is the case of an 1898 tale written by an American author named Morgan Andrew Robertson. A former sailor who struggled with alcoholism and poverty, Robertson got the ideas for his stories in a way that sounds a lot like Edgar Cayce's prophetic trances. Robertson would lie down and fall into partial consciousness. Stories would come to him in images like dreams or visions, and he would later write them down.

In one of these trances, Robertson saw a ship moving fast

through a night fog. It was huge, with more passengers than any ship Robertson had ever seen. A feeling of dread came over Robertson when he saw that the ship had only twenty-four lifeboats—not nearly enough. Then he saw an iceberg in the ship's path and, as the vision faded, he caught a glimpse of its name: *Titan*. From that disturbing vision, Robertson developed his story of the ship *Titan*, which grazed an iceberg in the North Atlantic Ocean and sank with great loss of life.

After the *Titanic* sank in 1912, scores of people claimed to have had premonitions of the tragedy.

Robertson's book was published under the title *Futility*. It didn't make much of a splash when it appeared, but fourteen years later, after the *Titanic* grazed an iceberg in the North Atlantic and sank with great loss of life, people started to see Robertson's book as a forecast of the disaster. There are about twenty striking similarities between the fictional ship and the real one, starting with their names. Other similarities include the size and passenger capacity of the two ships, the month of the accidents, the vessels' speed at the time of impact, the number of propellers, and the number of engines.

Today, Robertson's book is sold under the title *The Wreck of the Titan*, playing up its role as a prophecy of the *Titanic* disaster. Not everyone thinks that the book was prophetic, however. Science writer Martin Gardner, a skeptic about paranormal claims, wrote *The Wreck of the* Titanic *Foretold?* (1998) to debunk the "myth" that *Futility* predicted the *Titanic* disaster. Gardner argued that the similarities between the two ships and their fates could be explained by chance and by the fact that Robertson knew something about trends in shipbuilding and transatlantic shipping. As for the names, the Titans were giants in Greek mythology. The words *titan* and *titanic* refer to great size. In Gardner's view, it is not surprising that the creator of the *Titan* and the builders of the *Titanic* chose similar names—it's just a coincidence.

Harnessing the Power of Premonition

Anecdotes abound of individual lives saved by personal premonitions, such as, "I just had a feeling I shouldn't board that airplane!" If people do glimpse events to come, can their premonitions be used to prevent tragedies and save lives?

A few cases of prophecy have inspired large-scale public action, but these episodes have not been successes. When Edgar Cayce predicted that California would fall into the Pacific in the 1960s, some people moved out of the state—needlessly, as it turned out. In 1997 members of the American Heaven's Gate cult committed suicide because their leader had predicted that if they left their bodies they would be carried off by aliens arriving in a comet.

Suppose you had a strong premonition of disaster ahead but couldn't get anyone to listen! Cassandra, a woman in Greek mythology, suffered that frustrating fate. Apollo gave her the gift of prophecy, but when she refused to become his lover, he laid a curse upon her—she would still see the future, but no one would ever believe her.

Early in the twentieth century, an Irish aircraft engineer named John William Dunne had a dream in which he felt like a modern-day Cassandra. Dunne dreamed that he was on an island. The ground was steaming, and he realized that a volcano was about to erupt. He rushed about trying to persuade the French authorities on the island to evacuate the inhabitants. No one would listen.

A few days later Dunne saw a newspaper headline that read, "Volcano Disaster in Martinique. Town Swept Away. An Avalanche of Flame. Probable Loss of 40,000 Lives." Mount Pelée, a volcano on the French Caribbean island of Martinique, had erupted.

Some of Dunne's other dreams seemed prophetic, too. He foresaw a fire, an airplane accident, and a train wreck. Yet Dunne did not believe that he possessed psychic powers. Instead, he developed the idea that predictions were a form of time travel. Dunne described his theory in *An Experiment with Time* (1927). He believed that the mind of any dreamer can move through time, future as well as past. Dunne sug-

Aircraft engineer J. W. Dunne's prophetic dreams convinced him that precognition is a form of time travel.

gested that if people made a habit of carefully recording their dreams and comparing them with real-life events, many would find that some of their dreams contain previews of the future.

Dunne tried to explain premonitions and to study them systematically. Others have also tried to study the phenomenon of prediction and, if possible, use it to save lives. One such effort began after the collapse of a mine in the Welsh village of Aberfan killed more than a hundred schoolchildren in 1966. A London psychiatrist named J. C. Barker surveyed the public to see if anyone had had premonitions of the disaster. Some of the reports convinced Barker that precognition, or seeing things in advance, might be possible. In 1967 he set up a London office called the Premonitions Bureau. The next year a similar office, the Central Premonitions Registry, opened in the United States.

The goal of both groups was to collect written, dated premonitions from anyone who wanted to submit them. The premonitions were sorted into categories and compared with later events. If enough people reported similar-sounding premonitions of a coming disaster, the registry would issue an alert. Another benefit of the registries was that a string of successful predictions might indicate someone with psychic powers that could be studied in greater detail.

The Central Premonitions Registry's work was described in *Premonitions: A Leap into the Future,* by an American psychic researcher named Herbert Greenhouse. In 1971, when the book was published, the registry had about two thousand premonitions on file (some of the same premonitions had also been filed with the British bureau). Among the correct predictions Greenhouse reported were forecasts of the U.S. invasion of Cambodia, the death of Egyptian president Gamal Abdel Nasser, and the wreck of the Greek oil tanker *Arrow,* all in 1970.

Yet there were many predictions that failed, or that were too vague to be checked. The registries collected fewer reports than they had expected, and they found fewer significant hits than they had hoped for. Within a few years they stopped operating.

Today the Internet offers a fast, easy way for people from around the world to record premonitions. A number of Web sites have been set up to collect forecasts. If you have a dream that makes a powerful impression on you, one that leaves you with an urgent feeling that something is going to happen, you can search the Internet for places to leave a record of it. If your premonition turns out to be accurate, you'll be able to prove it—unless your premonition involves the destruction of the Internet.

Dreams that come true and premonitions of great events are spine-tinglingly fascinating. They stretch our imaginations and challenge our ideas about time, destiny, and the powers of the human mind. But how would you feel if someone foresaw your fate? If a friend or family member told you of a dream or vision in which you fell from a horse and were badly hurt, would you decide never to get on a horse . . . just in case?

James Randi, a professional magician and debunker
of paranormal and supernatural claims, offers a large prize
for proof of prophetic powers. No one has claimed it.

What Do You Think?

In the long history of human experience, it's likely that more people have believed in prophecy than have doubted it. The modern age, however, has cast scientific doubt on prophecy and the ancient arts of divination. Cold statistics paint a dismal picture for those who want to believe that we can see the future.

Researchers once studied 364 psychic predictions that had been published over four years in the *National Enquirer*. Four predictions had come true. "This means that the psychics—all of them top-rated professionals—were 98.9 percent wrong," James Randi wrote in *The Mask of Nostradamus*.

Astrology hasn't performed much better. In a study reported in *Nature* magazine in 1985, twenty-eight astrologers chosen by a San Francisco astrologers' association tried to match natal charts with detailed personality profiles. They got the matches right about a third of the time, about the same success rate that would be expected from random selections. Another study in 1987 gave charts prepared by astrologers to the subjects of the charts. Unknown to the subjects, half the charts had been reversed, which changed the astrological readings significantly. Yet as many people with reversed charts as with correct ones said that the charts accurately described them.

Many skeptics rule against the possibility of prediction because of results like these, together with known cases of fraud and the difficulty of proving even honest predictions. In fact, no form of prediction has been scientifically proven, with supporting evidence and statistics that rule out random chance. That doesn't mean, however, that prophecy will *never* be proven. Some researchers hope that further studies and more accurate record keeping will lead to a breakthrough.

But people who have had prophetic experiences might say that evidence and statistics don't matter. Even if the vast majority of predictions can't be proved, or can be shown to be hoaxes, one true prophecy could be considered a marvel.

Perhaps prophecy follows its own laws. If genuine glimpses of the future are buried among mistakes and delusions, prophecy's hits could be meaningful even when overwhelmed by misses. Science fiction writers have gone so far as to suggest that prophecy could be a form of communication between parallel universes, and that predictions that fail in this world come true on alternate earths.

Remember the Delphic oracle, one of history's best-known seers? Her reputation grew dim after the classical world of the Greeks and Romans came to an end around 500 CE. In 1892, French scientists investigated Delphi. They excavated the temple of Apollo, which had long been broken and buried, and found many of the things that had been described in ancient writings, even the Pythia's sacred *adyton*. One thing was missing: the chasm, or crack, in the rock floor. There was a spring of water, nothing more. The famous pneuma, the scientists concluded, was a myth. Maybe the prophecies, or even the oracle herself, were also myths, or frauds.

For about a century, people thought they knew the truth about Delphi. The mystery was gone. Then a geologist named Jelle de Boer and an archaeologist named John Hale looked at Delphi with new eyes. They found fault lines and other signs in the landscape that showed evidence of many earthquakes at Delphi over the years. In ancient times, the floor could have been cracked at the place where a spring now bubbled up. Fault lines that appear to pass through the ground beneath the temple contain petrochemicals that could have seeped into the *adyton* in the form of gases. Such natural deposits often give off ethylene, a sweet-smelling chemical that can produce intoxication and hallucinations. De Boer, Hale, and other researchers who joined their investigation began to think that they had found the source of the pneuma.

Suddenly there was a new explanation of the Delphic oracle's mysterious sayings: She had simply been high. But some of the recent investigators at Delphi think there may be more to the story. They suggest that the pneuma, coupled with the Pythia's religious belief in Apollo and her own powers of prediction, might have helped the oracle enter a mystical state of mind. If there is a kind of knowledge not available to reason, perhaps she was able to grasp it from time to time, just long enough to utter the prophecies that made Delphi famous for a thousand years.

The sacred vapor, secret of the Pythia's power, may have been an intoxicating gas breathed forth by the earth.

No one can prove that prophecy exists, just as no one can prove that it doesn't. You'll have to decide for yourself whether, in the words of the writer Joseph Conrad, "The mind of man is capable of anything—because everything is in it, all the past as well as all the future."

Glossary

astrology Belief that the positions and movements of the planets affect human life; the practice of foretelling someone's future based on those movements.

augury Foretelling the future through signs; the foreteller is called an augur.

debunk To prove that a supernatural or paranormal claim is false, or at least suspicious, by providing a natural explanation, pointing out holes or weaknesses in the claim, or exposing a hoax.

divination Originally, finding the will of the gods; now used more generally to mean fortune-telling, or seeing the future.

necromancy Communication with the spirits of the dead for purposes of gaining knowledge; sometimes linked to sinful or forbidden knowledge, or practices such as sorcery or black magic.

omen Event or object that is a sign of future happenings.

oracle One who is believed to have mystical or supernatural powers to answer questions or predict the future.

phenomenon Something unusual or remarkable.

precognition Knowledge of the future.

premonition A feeling of fear or warning that something is going to happen.

prophecy A foretelling of the future, often linked to religious belief or ceremony.

psychic One who has, or claims to have, paranormal or supernatural powers, such as seeing the future or reading minds.

skeptic One who requires extraordinary proof of extraordinary claims and uses critical thinking to test statements.

sortilege Foretelling the future in the chance arrangement of manipulated objects, such as lots, cards, or sticks.

For Further Research

Books

Blackwood, Gary L. *Fateful Forebodings*. New York: Benchmark Books, 1999.

*Gallant, Roy. *Astrology: Sense or Nonsense?* Garden City, NY: Doubleday, 1974.

Hall, Judy. *Divination: A Practical Guide to Predicting the Future*. New York: Godsfield, 2000.

Krull, Kathleen. *They Saw the Future: Oracles, Psychics, Scientists, Great Thinkers, and Pretty Good Guessers*. New York: Atheneum, 1999.

Landau, Elaine. *Fortune-Telling*. Brookfield, CT: Millbrook, 1996.

Time-Life Books. *Visions and Prophecies*. Mysteries of the Unknown series. Alexandria, VA: Time-Life, 1988.

Web Sites

www.skepdic.com/oracles.html
> **The Skeptic's Dictionary* is an Internet reference that covers supernatural and paranormal topics "from abracadabra to zombies." Its "Oracles" page briefly defines *prophecy* and provides links to more detailed coverage under such topics as divination, Jeane Dixon, Mayan prophecy, and Nostradamus. *The Skeptic's Dictionary* also offers a set of mini lessons in critical thinking.

http://news.nationalgeographic.com/news/2001/08/0814_delphioracle.html
> This *National Geographic* news article summarizes the theory that the oracle of Delphi may have inhaled natural vapors. This Web page has links to other sources of information about Delphi and the oracle.

www.infoplease.com/spot/astrology1.html
> "Cosmic Counsel" provides a brief overview of astrology and the arguments for it and against it. It also explores why people are drawn to astrology.

www.isidore-of-seville.com/astdiv/
> *Ancient Divination and Astrology on the Web* is a doorway to several hundred Internet pages about prophecy and fortune-telling in the ancient world,

---

*Book or Web site that will help develop critical thinking

especially in Greece and Rome. Each link has a brief description. The focus is on the role of prophecy in society and culture.

www.activemind.com/Mysterious/Topics/Nostradamus/index.html
This kid-friendly "Could He See the Future?" page about Nostradamus offers a quatrain for study and testing, a time line, and links to a short biography and to other sites written by both believers and skeptics.

*www.randi.org/index.html
The James Randi Educational Foundation maintains this site, created by professional magician and paranormal skeptic James Randi. It has many resources for people interested in the investigative approach to prophecy. One of them is the full text of Randi's encyclopedia of the occult and supernatural, where you can look up such subjects as Nostradamus, prophecy, and astrology.

www.mainportals.com/precog.shtml
This new online version of the Central Premonitions Registry accepts reports of dreams, visions, prophecies, or premonitions so that they can be checked against later events.

http://rinkworks.com/said/predictions.shtml
The "Bad Predictions" page of a site called *Things People Said* lists statements and predictions that later turned out to be wrong, wrong, wrong. Although no sources are provided for checking the facts, some of the bad predictions are reported elsewhere, and many are entertaining.

Selected Bibliography

The author found these resources especially helpful when researching and writing this book.

Allan, Tony. *Prophecies: 4,000 Years of Prophets, Visionaries, and Predictions.* London: Thorsons, 2002.

Ashe, Geoffrey. *The Book of Prophecy: From Ancient Greece to the Millennium.* London: Blandford, 1999.

——————. *The Encyclopedia of Prophecy.* Santa Barbara, CA: ABC-Clio, 2001.

Boyer, Paul. *When Time Shall Be No More: Prophecy Belief in Modern American Culture.* Cambridge, MA: Harvard University Press, 1992.

Broad, William J. *The Oracle: The Lost Secrets and Hidden Message of Ancient Delphi.* New York: Penguin, 2006.

Fiery, Ann. *The Book of Divination.* New York: Chronicle, 1999.

Gardner, Martin, ed. *The Wreck of the* Titanic *Foretold?* Amherst, NY: Prometheus, 1998.

Lemesurier, Peter. *The Nostradamus Encyclopedia.* New York: St. Martin's, 1997.

Lewis, James. *Doomsday Prophecies: A Complete Guide to the End of the World.* Amherst, MA: Prometheus, 2000.

Loewe, Michael, and Carmen Blacker, eds. *Divination and Oracles.* London: George Allen & Unwin, 1981.

Matthews, John, ed. *The World Atlas of Divination.* London: BCA, 1992.

Parke, H. W. *Sibyls and Sibylline Prophecy in Classical Antiquity.* New York: Routledge, 1992.

Pickover, Clifford A. *Dreaming the Future: The Fantastic Story of Prediction.* Amherst, NY: Prometheus, 2001.

Randi, James. *The Mask of Nostradamus: A Biography of the World's Most Famous Prophet.* New York: Scribner's, 1990.

Sherden, William A. *The Fortune Sellers: The Big Business of Buying and Selling Predictions.* New York: Wiley, 1999.

Stewart, J. V. *Astrology: What's Really in the Stars.* Amherst, NY: Prometheus, 1996.

Notes

Is It True?

Croesus and the Delphic oracle from William J. Broad, *The Oracle: The Lost Secrets and Hidden Message of Ancient Delphi*, New York: Penguin, 2006, pp. 51–54, and Tony Allan, *Prophecies: 4,000 Years of Prophets, Visionaries, and Predictions*, London: Thorsons, 2002, pp. 24–27. Pausanias and Lebadea from Broad, p. 52, and Allan, p. 23. Plato and prophecy from Allan, pp. 22–23. Brahan Seer from Allan, pp. 124–125; Clifford A. Pickover, *Dreaming the Future: The Fantastic Story of Prediction*, Amherst, NY: Prometheus, 2001, pp. 274–276; and Glass, Justine, *They Foresaw the Future: The Story of Fulfilled Prophecy*, New York: Putnam's, 1969, pp. 130–140.

Chapter 1: Prophets, Oracles, Sibyls, and Seers

Biblical references from New Jerusalem Bible, Garden City, NY: Doubleday, 1966. Delphic oracle's influence from William J. Broad, *The Oracle: The Lost Secrets and Hidden Message of Ancient Delphi*, New York: Penguin, 2006, p. 11. Oracle's prophecies from Broad, pp. 56–57, 71, and Pickover, pp. 229–231. Maya calendar from Canadian Museum of Civilization, "The Maya Calendar," at www.civilization.ca/civil/maya/mmc06eng.html and Allan, pp. 94–95.

Chapter 2: Reading the Signs

Magellan from Allan, p. 75, and Rebecca Stefoff, *Ferdinand Magellan and the Discovery of the World Ocean*, New York: Chelsea House, 1990, p. 97. Louis XI and Cardano anecdotes from Pickover, p. 107. Tarot from James Randi Educational Foundation at www.randi.org/encyclopedia/Tarot%20cards.html; *The Skeptic's Dictionary* at www.skepdic.com/tarot.html; Pickover, pp. 137–146; and Allan, pp. 88–91.

Chaper 3: Visions of the Future

Parade quote from C. Eugene Emery Jr., "When the Media Tell Half the Story," *Skeptical Inquirer*, May/June 1997 at www.csicop.org/si/0705/media-watch.html, and Straight Dope Science Advisory Board at www.straightdope.com/mailbag/mdixon.html. Quote about Kennedy from Clifford A. Pickover, *Dreaming the Future: The Fantastic Story of Prediction*, Amherst, NY: Prometheus, 2001, p. 315, and *The Skeptic's Dictionary* at www.skepdic.com/dixon.html.

Dixon predictions from Pickover, pp. 315–316; Justine Glass, *They Foresaw the Future*, New York: Putnam's, 1969, pp. 223–228; and Emery. "Jeane Dixon effect" from "Psychic Jeane Dixon Dies" at www.cnn.com/showbiz/9701/26/dixon.html. Nostradamus quatrains translated by the author from the French versions given in Peter Lemesurier, *The Nostradamus Encyclopedia*, New York: St. Martin's, 1997. Shipton prophecies quoted in Pickover, pp. 238–239.

Chapter 4: Dreams and Premonitions

Hitler quote from Walter S. Frank, "Adolf Hitler: The Making of a Fuhrer" at www.smoter.com/abornsol/html. Lincoln quote from "Lincoln's Premonition" at www.paranormal.about.com/library/weekly/aa022100a.htm. Williams anecdote from Tony Allan, *Prophecies: 4,000 Years of Prophets, Visionaries, and Predictions*, London: Thorsons, 2002, p. 64. *Titanic* and *Titan* comparison from Clifford A. Pickover, *Dreaming the Future: The Fantastic Story of Prediction*, Amherst, NY: Prometheus, 2001, pp. 216–218. Martinique headline from Allan, p. 69.

What Do You Think?

Randi quote from James Randi, *The Mask of Nostradamus: A Biography of the World's Most Famous Prophet*, New York: Scribner's, 1990, p. 31. Astrology failures in Shawn Carlson, "A Double-Blind Test of Astrology," *Nature*, 318, 419, 1985, and Geoffrey Dean, "Does Astrology Need to Be True? Part 1: A Look at the Real Thing," *Skeptical Inquirer* 11, no. 2 (Winter 1987); both cited in Clifford A. Pickover, *Dreaming the Future: The Fantastic Story of Prediction*, Amherst, NY: Prometheus, 2001, p. 117. Delphi from William J. Broad, *The Oracle: The Lost Secrets and Hidden Message of Ancient Delphi*, New York: Penguin, 2006.

Index

Page numbers for illustrations are in boldface

About the Author

Rebecca Stefoff's many books for young readers cover a wide range of topics in science, history, and literature. Scary stories and vampire movies are among her favorite entertainments. As a member of CSICOP (the Committee for the Scientific Investigation of Claims of the Paranormal), Stefoff supports a thoughtful, research-based approach to supernatural and paranormal subjects. She lives in Portland, Oregon.